Contents

MacCAIG · MORGAN · LOCHHEAD

—

THREE
SCOTTISH POETS

—

Edited and introduced by

R.   Za

CANONGATE
CLASSICS
45

This selection first published as a Canongate Classic in 1992. Reprinted in 1995 by Canongate Books Ltd, 14 The High Street, Edinburgh. Notes and introductions © Roderick Watson 1992. All rights reserved.

Reprinted 1998

Poems by Norman MacCaig appear in this selection by kind permission of Chatto & Windus. Poems by Edwin Morgan appear in this selection by kind permission of Carcanet Press Ltd. and Ian McKelvie. Poems by Liz Lochhead appear in this selection by kind permission of Polygon.

The publishers gratefully acknowledge general subsidy from the Scottish Arts Council towards the Canongate Classics series and a specific grant towards the publication of this volume.

CANONGATE CLASSICS
Series Editor: Roderick Watson
Editorial Board: Tom Crawford, J.B. Pick

British Library Cataloguing-in-Publication Data
A catalogue record for this book is available on request from the British Library.

ISBN 0 86241 400 8

Typeset by Wordpower, Berwickshire
Printed and bound in Finland by WSOY.

Norman MacCaig

BORN IN EDINBURGH in 1910, Norman MacCaig was educated at the Royal High School and Edinburgh University where he took an Honours degree in Classics, graduating in 1932. After training as a schoolteacher he has followed the profession and lived in Edinburgh for most of his life. He married his wife Isabel in 1940 and they raised a family of two children. When war broke out a deeply held personal conviction against killing led MacCaig to become a conscientious objector and he passed the war years in non-military work, but not before undergoing a spell in prison for his beliefs. He became the first writer in residence at Edinburgh University between 1967 and 1969; and in 1970 he went on to work for eight years as a regular member of staff, and later as a Reader, in the English Department at the University of Stirling. The Queen's Medal for Poetry is among the many honours he has since received. Sixteen books of his poetry have appeared between 1943 and 1988, and an expanded edition of his *Collected Poems* marked his eightieth birthday in 1990.

MacCaig's first poems appeared in the periodicals of the thirties and forties, and were associated with the New Apocalypse movement. He has since disowned his first two collections, however, as unnecessarily obscure. Clarity, simplicity and a classical balance have characterised his work ever since, but the interest in landscape was there from the first, and a questing, wry, metaphysically speculative, witty and sceptical turn of mind has been an equally constant quality.

In poem after poem throughout his long career MacCaig has celebrated the physical world—memorably realised in the particular details of landscape, or in the smaller animals which inhabit it—to give us life, delight and sheer surprise, seen for example in 'Toad', 'Vestey's Well' and 'Basking Shark'. In this respect MacCaig has something in common with the Gaelic tradition of praise poems, and indeed he has kept in touch with his mother's Highland roots—she came from Scalpay, Harris— by spending the summer months of almost every year in Inverkirkaig, to the south of Lochinver on the west coast.

Poems such as 'Crofter's Kitchen: Evening', 'Return to Scalpay', 'A Man in Assynt', 'Aunt Julia', 'Among Scholars', and the moving sequence 'Poems for Angus', all speak of MacCaig's love for Highland Scotland, the people he knows there, and the modest but enduring values of common wisdom, community and care which they embody. By the same token he has had a life-long hatred of hypocrisy, cant, pretension and cruelty; nor does he turn his eyes away from the suffering or the inequalities to be found in the world ('Visiting Hour', 'Assisi', 'Blind Horse' and 'Two Thieves'). Perhaps MacCaig's finest achievement has been to unite all these elements of his vision in poems which combine wit, wry humour and celebration with an essentially tragic recognition of how quickly life passes. This recognition is usually implicit and never solemn, but the compassion and the grace to be found in poems such as 'Memorial', 'Incident', 'Notations of Ten Summer Minutes' and 'Water Tap' have given us some of the finest short lyrics of our time.

AFTER

Let's choose a pretty word, say, *evening,*
And climb through it into the past,
Or stand on a towering If, surveying
The rosy kingdoms we have lost.

From every corner creep a thousand
Boredoms saying, *Greet us. We're life.*
Let's round the sunset up and milk it
Into a jug and drink it off.

Or in the hawthorn let us tangle
Our dreary look like gossamer
To shudder with that sparrow's chirping
And when the dew falls be on fire.

Or drag the distance home and chain it
There in the corner of the room
To charm us with its savage howling
And beg for fragments of our dream.

There's a clue somewhere. Can you find it?
Can you say over and over again
'Love', till its incantation makes us
Forget how much we are alone?

SUMMER FARM

Straws like tame lightnings lie about the grass
And hang zigzag on hedges. Green as glass
The water in the horse-trough shines.
Nine ducks go wobbling by in two straight lines.

A hen stares at nothing with one eye,
Then picks it up. Out of an empty sky
A swallow falls and, flickering through
The barn, dives up again into the dizzy blue.

I lie, not thinking, in the cool, soft grass,
Afraid of where a thought might take me—as
This grasshopper with plated face
Unfolds his legs and finds himself in space.

Self under self, a pile of selves I stand
Threaded on time, and with metaphysic hand
Lift the farm like a lid and see
Farm within farm, and in the centre, me.

FEEDING DUCKS

One duck stood on my toes.
The others made watery rushes after bread
Thrown by my momentary hand; instead,
She stood duck-still and got far more than those.

An invisible drone boomed by
With a beetle in it; the neighbour's yearning bull
Bugled across five fields. And an evening full
Of other evenings quietly began to die.

And my everlasting hand
Dropped on my hypocrite duck her grace of bread.
And I thought, 'The first to be fattened, the first to be dead',
Till my gestures enlarged, wide over the darkening land.

BYRE

The thatched roof rings like heaven where mice
Squeak small hosannahs all night long,
Scratching its golden pavements, skirting
The gutter's crystal river-song.

Wild kittens in the world below
Glare with one flaming eye through cracks,
Spurt in the straw, are tawny brooches
Splayed on the chests of drunken sacks.

The dimness becomes darkness as
Vast presences come mincing in,
Swagbellied Aphrodites, swinging
A silver slaver from each chin.

And all is milky, secret, female.
Angels are hushed and plain straws shine.
And kittens miaow in circles, stalking
With tail and hindleg one straight line.

A MAN I AGREED WITH

He knew better than to admire a chair
and say *What does it mean?*

He loved everything that accepted
the unfailing hospitality of his five senses.
He would say *Hello, caterpillar* or
So long, Loch Fewin.

He wanted to know
how they came to be what they are:
But he never insulted them by saying
Caterpillar, Loch Fewin, what do you mean?

In this respect he was like God,
though he was godless.—He knew the difference
between *What does it mean to me?*
and *What does it mean?*

That's why he said, half smiling,
Of course, God, like me,
is an atheist.

INTERRUPTION TO A JOURNEY

The hare we had run over
bounced about the road
on the springing curve
of its spine.

Cornfields breathed in the darkness.
We were going through the darkness and
the breathing cornfields from one
important place to another.

We broke the hare's neck
and made that place, for a moment,
the most important place there was,
where a bowstring was cut
and a bow broken for ever
that had shot itself through so many
darknesses and cornfields.

It was left in that landscape.
It left us in another.

VISITING HOUR

The hospital smell
combs my nostrils
as they go bobbing along
green and yellow corridors.

What seems a corpse
is trundled into a lift and vanishes
heavenward.

I will not feel, I will not
feel, until
I have to.

Nurses walk lightly, swiftly,
here and up and down and there,
their slender waists miraculously
carrying their burden
of so much pain, so
many deaths, their eyes
still clear after
so many farewells.

Ward 7. She lies
in a white cave of forgetfulness.
A withered hand
trembles on its stalk. Eyes move
behind eyelids too heavy
to raise. Into an arm wasted
of colour a glass fang is fixed,
not guzzling but giving.
And between her and me

distance shrinks till there is none left
but the distance of pain that neither she nor I
can cross.

She smiles a little at this
black figure in her white cave
who clumsily rises
in the round swimming waves of a bell
and dizzily goes off, growing fainter,
not smaller, leaving behind only
books that will not be read
and fruitless fruits.

ASSISI

The dwarf with his hands on backwards
sat, slumped like a half-filled sack
on tiny twisted legs from which
sawdust might run,
outside the three tiers of churches built
in honour of St Francis, brother
of the poor, talker with birds, over whom
he had the advantage
of not being dead yet.

A priest explained
how clever it was of Giotto
to make his frescoes tell stories
that would reveal to the illiterate the goodness
of God and the suffering
of His Son. I understood
the explanation and
the cleverness.

A rush of tourists, clucking contentedly,
fluttered after him as he scattered
the grain of the Word. It was they who had passed
the ruined temple outside, whose eyes
wept pus, whose back was higher
than his head, whose lopsided mouth
said *Grazie* in a voice as sweet
as a child's when she speaks to her mother
or a bird's when it spoke
to St Francis.

BLIND HORSE

He snuffles towards
pouches of water in the grass
and doesn't drink
when he finds them.

He twitches listlessly
at sappy grass stems and stands
stone still, his hanging head
caricatured with a scribble
of green whiskers.

Sometimes that head swings high,
ears cock—and he stares
down a long sound,
he stares and whinnies
for what never comes.

His eyes never close,
not in the heat of the day
when his leather lip droops and
he wears blinkers of flies.

At any time of the night
you hear him in his dark field
stamp the ground, stamp
the world down, waiting impatiently
for the light to break.

TWO FOCUSES

Blind worm, lasciviously stroking yourself through
damp grass, do you think to escape
the springheeled thrush or the wren,
that fusspot in green hedges?

Brown water, you'll lose
that peat stain, your throat
will be choked with salt, you
will entertain monsters.

Red stag, you'll be an old rug rotting in the heather,
or a bullet
will drop the whole world away
from under your feet.
Such dooms, and nothing to tremble for them
but the one human figure in the landscape
who, because he trembles for them,
is the one intruder.

I tremble for them. But death shrinks back again
into the beautiful forms of his disguises.
And I see only that mountain, this stream,
this pool, clipped between rocks like an agate.
And death and history hide behind
a rowan branch that
drags and skips and drags and skips
on the brown glass of water—on it
spin Christmas roses of foam.

From 'Poems for Angus'

NOTES ON A WINTER JOURNEY
AND A FOOTNOTE

1

The snow's almost faultless. It bounces back
the sun's light but can do nothing with
those two stags, their cold noses, their yellow teeth.

2

On the loch's eye a cataract is forming.
Fistfuls of white make the telephone wires
loop after loop of snow buntings.

3

So few cars, they leave the snow snow.
I think of the horrible marzipan
in the streets of Edinburgh.

4

The hotel at Ullapool, that should be a bang of light,
is crepuscular. The bar is fireflied
with whisky glasses.

5

At Inchnadamph snow is falling. The windscreen wipers
squeak and I stare through
a segment of a circle. What more do I ever do? . . .

6

(Seventeen miles to go. I didn't know it, but when
I got there a death waited for me—that segment
shut its fan: and a blinding winter closed in.)

A.K. MACLEOD

I went to the landscape I love best
and the man who was its meaning and added to it
met me at Ullapool.

The beautiful landscape was under snow
and was beautiful in a new way.

Next morning, the man who had greeted me
with the pleasure of pleasure
vomited blood
and died.

Crofters and fishermen and womenfolk, unable
to say any more, said,
'It's a grand day, it's a beautiful day.'

And I thought, 'Yes, it is.'
And I thought of him lying there,
the dead centre of it all.

BLACKBIRD IN A SUNSET BUSH

Everything's in the sunset. Windows
flare in it, rooms blush.
Cars scatter everywhere—they make the city
one huge pintable. Life is opulent
as thunder.

Only the blackbird there
contemplates
what the sunset's in:
what makes a flower ponderous
and breathes a mountain away.

The gravity of beauty—
how thoughtfully, how pensively he puts it,
charcoal philosopher
in his blazing study.

INEDUCABLE ME

I don't learn much, I'm a man
of no improvements. My nose still snuffs the air
in an amateurish way. My profoundest ideas
were once toys on the floor, I love them, I've licked
most of the paint off. A whisky glass
is a rattle I don't shake. When I love
a person, a place, an object, I don't see
what there is to argue about.

I learned words, I learned words: but half of them
died for lack of exercise. And the ones I use
often look at me
with a look that whispers, *Liar*.

How I admire the eider duck that dives
with a neat loop and no splash and the gannet that suddenly
harpoons the sea.—I'm a guillemot
that still dives
in the first way it thought of: poke your head under
and fly down.

BASKING SHARK

To stub an oar on a rock where none should be,
To have it rise with a slounge out of the sea
Is a thing that happened once (too often) to me.

But not too often—though enough. I count as gain
That once I met, on a sea tin-tacked with rain,
That roomsized monster with a matchbox brain.

He displaced more than water. He shoggled me
Centuries back—this decadent townee
Shook on a wrong branch of his family tree.

Swish up the dirt and, when it settles, a spring
Is all the clearer. I saw me, in one fling,
Emerging from the slime of everything.

So who's the monster? The thought made me grow pale
For twenty seconds while, sail after sail,
The tall fin slid away and then the tail.

FROGS

Frogs sit more solid
than anything sits. In mid-leap they are
parachutists falling
in a free fall. They die on roads
with arms across their chests and
heads high.

I love frogs that sit
like Buddha, that fall without
parachutes, that die
like Italian tenors.

Above all, I love them because,
pursued in water, they never
panic so much that they fail
to make stylish triangles
with their ballet dancer's
legs.

TOAD

Stop looking like a purse. How could a purse
squeeze under the rickety door and sit,
full of satisfaction, in a man's house?

You clamber towards me on your four corners—
right hand, left foot, left hand, right foot.

I love you for being a toad,
for crawling like a Japanese wrestler,
and for not being frightened.

I put you in my purse hand, not shutting it,
and set you down outside directly under
every star.

A jewel in your head? Toad,*
you've put one in mine,
a tiny radiance in a dark place.

*Legend has it that toads have a jewel in their foreheads.

MY LAST WORD ON FROGS

People have said to me, *You seem to like frogs.*
They keep jumping into your poems.

I do. I love the way they sit,
compact as a cat and as indifferent
to everything but style, like a lady remembering
to keep her knees together. And I love
the elegant way they jump and
the inelegant way they land.
So human.

I feel so close to them
I must be froggish myself.
I look in the mirror expecting to see
a fairytale Prince.

But no. It's just sprawling me,
croaking away
and swivelling my eyes around
for the stealthy heron and his stabbing beak.

CROSSING THE BORDER

I sit with my back to the engine, watching
the landscape pouring away out of my eyes.
I think I know where I'm going and have
some choice in the matter.

I think, too, that this was a country
of bog-trotters, moss-troopers,
fired ricks and roof-trees in the black night—glinting
on tossed horns and red blades.
I think of lives
bubbling into the harsh grass.

What difference now?
I sit with my back to the future, watching
time pouring away into the past. I sit, being helplessly
lugged backwards
through the Debatable Lands of history, listening
to the execrations, the scattered cries, the
falling of roof-trees
in the lamentable dark.

CROFTER'S KITCHEN: EVENING

A man's boots with a woman in them
Clatter across the floor. A hand
Long careless of the lives it kills
Comes down and thwacks on newspapers
A long black fish with bloody gills.

The kettle's at her singsong—minor
Prophetess in her sooty cave.
A kitten climbs the bundled net
On the bench and, curled up like a cowpat,
Purrs on the *Stornoway Gazette.*

The six hooks of a Mackerel Dandy
Climb their thin rope—an exclamation
By the curled question of a gaff.
Three rubber eels cling like a crayfish
On top of an old photograph.

Peats fur themselves in gray. The door
Bursts open, chairs creak, a hand reaches out
For spectacles, a lamp flares high . . .
The collie underneath the table
Slumps with a world-rejecting sigh.

RETURN TO SCALPAY

The ferry wades across the kyle. I drive
The car ashore
On to a trim tarred road. A car on Scalpay?
Yes, and a road where never was one before.
The ferryman's Gaelic wonders who I am
(Not knowing I know it), this man back from the dead,
Who takes the blue-black road (no traffic jam)
From by Craig Lexie over to Bay Head.

A man bows in the North wind, shaping up
His lazybeds,
And through the salt air vagrant peat smells waver
From houses where no house should be. The sheds
At the curing station have been newly tarred.
Aunt Julia's house has vanished. The Red Well
Has been bulldozed away. But sharp and hard
The church still stands, barring the road to Hell.

A chugging prawn boat slides round Cuddy Point
Where in a gale
I spread my batwing jacket and jumped farther
Than I've jumped since. There's where I used to sail
Boats looped from rushes. On the jetty there
I caught eels, cut their heads off and watched them slew
Slow through the water. Ah—Cape Finisterre
I called that point, to show how much I knew.

While Hamish sketches, a crofter tells me that
The Scalpay folk,
Though very intelligent, are not Spinozas ...
We walk the Out End road (no need to invoke
That troublemaker, Memory, she's everywhere)

To Laggandoan, greeted all the way—
My city eyeballs prickle; it's hard to bear
With such affection and such gaiety.

Scalpay revisited?—more than Scalpay. I
Have no defence,
For half my thought and half my blood is Scalpay,
Against that pure, hardheaded innocence
That shows love without shame, weeps without shame,
Whose every thought is hospitality—

Edinburgh, Edinburgh, you're dark years away.
Scuttering snowflakes riddling the hard wind
Are almost spent
When we reach Johann's house. She fills the doorway,
Sixty years of size and astonishment,
Then laughs and cries and laughs, as she always did
And will (Easy glum, easy glow, a friend would say) . . .
Scones, oatcakes, herrings from under a bubbling lid.
Then she comes with us to put us on our way.

Hugging my arm in her stronger one, she says,
Fancy me
Walking this road beside my darling Norman!
And what is there to say? . . . We look back and see
Her monumental against the flying sky
And I am filled with love and praise and shame
Knowing that I have been, and knowing why,
Diminished and enlarged. Are they the same?

An old song. A rickle of stones. A
name on a map.
I read on a map a name whose Gaelic means
the Battlefield of the Big Men.
I think of yelling hosts, banners,
counterattacks, deployments. When I get there,
it's ten acres, ten small acres
of boggy ground.
I feel
I am looking through the same wrong end
of the same telescope
through which I look back through time
and see
Christ, Socrates, Dante—all the Big Men
picked out, on their few acres,
clear and tiny in
the misty landscape of history.

Up from that mist crowds
the present. This day has lain long,
and dozed late, till
the church bell jerks and, wagging madly
in its salty tower, sends its voice
clanking through the sabbath drowse.
And dark minds in black clothes gather like
bees to the hive, to share
the bitter honey of the Word, to submit
to the hard judgement of a God
my childhood God would have a difficulty
in recognising.
Ten yards from the sea's surge

they sing to Him beautiful praises
that surge like the sea,
in a bare stone box built
for the worship of the Creator
of all colours and between-colours, and of
all shapes, and of the holiness
of identity and of the purifying light-stream
of reason. The sound of that praise
escapes from the stone box
and takes its place in the ordinary communion
of all sounds, that are
Being expressing itself—as it does in its continuous,
its never-ending creation of leaves,
birds, waves, stone boxes—and beliefs,
the true and the false.

These shapes, these incarnations, have their own determined
identities, their own dark holiness, their
high absurdities. See how they make
a breadth and assemblage of animals,
a perpendicularity of creatures, from where,
three thousand feet up, two ravens go by
in their seedy, nonchalant way, down to
the burn-mouth where baby mussels
drink fresh water through their beards—
or down, down still, to where the masked conger eel
goes like a gangster through
the weedy slums at the sea's foot.

Greenshank, adder, wildcat, guillemot, seatrout,
fox and falcon—the list winds through
all the crooks and crannies of this landscape, all
the subtleties and shifts of its waters and

the prevarications of its air—
while roofs fall in, walls crumble, gables
die last of all, and man becomes,
in this most beautiful corner of the land,
one of the rare animals.

Up there, the scraping light
whittles the cloud edges till, like thin bone,
they're bright with their own opaque selves. Down here,
a skinny rosebush is an eccentric jug
of air. They make me,
somewhere between them,
a visiting eye,
an unrequited passion,
watching the tide glittering backward and making
its huge withdrawal from beaches
and kilted rocks. And the mind
behind the eye, within the passion,
remembers with certainty that the tide will return
and thinks, with hope, that that other ebb,
that sad withdrawal of people, may, too,
reverse itself and flood
the bays and the sheltered glens
with new generations replenishing the land
with its richest of riches and coming, at last,
into their own again.

TWO THIEVES

At the Place for Pulling up Boats
(one word in Gaelic) the tide is full.
It seeps over the grass, stealthy as a robber.
Which it is.

—For old Flora tells me
that fifty yards stretch of gravel, now under water,
was, in her granny's time, a smooth green sward
where the Duke of Sutherland
turned his coach and four.

What an image of richness, a tiny pageantry
in this small dying place
whose every house is now lived in
by the sad widow of a fine strong man.

There were fine strong men in the Duke's time.
He drove them to the shore, he drove them
to Canada. He gave no friendly thought to them
as he turned his coach and four
on the sweet green sward
by the Place for Pulling up Boats
where no boats are.

AUNT JULIA

Aunt Julia spoke Gaelic
very loud and very fast.
I could not answer her—
I could not understand her.

She wore men's boots
when she wore any.
—I can see her strong foot,
stained with peat,
paddling with the treadle of the spinningwheel
while her right hand drew yarn
marvellously out of the air.

Hers was the only house
where I've lain at night
in the absolute darkness
of a box bed, listening to
crickets being friendly.

She was buckets
and water flouncing into them.
She was winds pouring wetly
round house-ends.
She was brown eggs, black skirts
and a keeper of threepennybits
in a teapot.

Aunt Julia spoke Gaelic
very loud and very fast.
By the time I had learned
a little, she lay

silenced in the absolute black
of a sandy grave
at Luskentyre.
But I hear her still, welcoming me
with a seagull's voice
across a hundred yards
of peatscrapes and lazybeds
and getting angry, getting angry
with so many questions
unanswered.

COUNTRY DANCE

The room whirled and coloured
and figured itself with dancers.
Another gaiety seemed born of theirs
and flew like streamers
between their heads and the ceiling.

I gazed, coloured and figured,
down the tunnel of streamers—
and there, in the band, an old fiddler
sawing away in the privacy
of music. He bowed lefthanded and his right hand
was the wrong way round. Impossible.
But the jig bounced, the gracenotes
sparkled on the surface of the tune.
The odd man out, when it came to music,
was the odd man in.

There's a lesson here, I thought, climbing
into the pulpit I keep in my mind.
But before I'd said *Firstly brethren*, the tune
ended, the dancers parted, the old fiddler
took a cigarette from the pianist, stripped off
the paper and ate the tobacco.

AMONG SCHOLARS

On our way to a loch, two miles from Inveruplan,
Three of us (keepers) read the landscape as
I read a book. They missed no word of it:
Fox-hole, strange weed, blue berry, ice-scrape, deer's hoof-print.
It was their back yard, and fresh as the garden in Eden
(Striped rock 'like a belted Galloway'). They saw what I
Saw, and more, and its meaning. They spoke like a native
The language they walked in. I envied them, naturally.

Coming back, we dragged the boat down to Inveruplan,
Lurching and slithering, both it and us. A stag
Paused in the thickening light to see that strange thing,
A twelve-legged boat in a bog. Angie roared at it
Like a stag in rut. Denying its other senses
It came and paused and came—and took itself off,
A text, a chapter and verse, into its gospel.
We took up the rope and hauled on, sweating and gasping.

We left the boat in the hayfield at Inveruplan:
The tractor would get it. A moon was coming up
Over the roof and under it a Tilley lamp
Hissed in its yellow self. We took our noise
Into the room and shut it in with us
Where, till light broke on a boat foundered in dew,
I drank down drams in a company of scholars
With exploding songs and a three-days ache in my shoulder.

VESTEY'S WELL*

We raised the lid. The cold spring water was
So clear it wasn't there.
At the foot of its non-depth a grave toad squatted
As still as Buddha in his non-place. Flaws
Breathed on the water—he trembled to no-where
Then steadied into being again. A fretted
Fern was his Bo-tree. Time in that delicate place
Sat still for ever staring in its own place.

We filled the jam-jar with bright nothing and
Drank down its freezing light
That the sun burned us with (that raging planet
That will not stand and will not understand)
And tried to feel we were each one a bright
And delicate place with a philosopher in it—
And failed; and let the hinged lid slowly fall.
The little Buddha hadn't moved at all.

*The Vestey family own large estates in Assynt.

They sprint eight feet and—
stop. Like that. They
sprintayard (like that) and
stop.
They have no acceleration
and no brakes.
Top speed's their only one.

They're alive—put life
through a burning-glass, they're
its focus—but they share
the world of delicate clockwork.

In spasmodic
Indian file
they parallel the parallel ripples.

When they stop
they, suddenly,
are gravel.

STILL LIFE

Three apples, if they are apples, and a jug,
A lemon (certain), grapes, a fish's tail,
A melting fruitdish and a randy table:
Squared off from other existences they struggle
Into a peace, a balancing of such power
As past and future use in being Now.

Still life, they call it—like a bursting bomb
That keeps on bursting, one burst, on and on:
A new existence, continually being born,
Emerging out of white into the sombre
Garishness of the spectrum, refusing the easy,
Clenching its strength on nothing but how to be.

Nice lesson for a narrative or for
A thing made emblem—that martyrs in their fire,
Christs on their crosses, fêtes and massacres,
When purified of their small history,
Cannot surpass, no matter how they struggle,
Three apples (more than likely) and a jug.

MUTUAL LIFE

A wildcat, furfire in a bracken bush,
Twitches his club-tail, rounds his amber eyes
At rockabye rabbits humped on the world. The air
Crackles about him. His world is a rabbit's size.

And in milky pearls, in a liquefaction of green,
One of ten thousand, spattering squabs of light,
A mackerel shuttles the hanging waterwebs,
Muscling through tons, slipping them left and right.

What do you know, mind, of that speck in air,
The high insanitary raven that pecks his claws
A thousand feet up and volplanes on his back
And greets his ancient sweetheart with coarse caws?

You tell a hand to rise and you think it yours.
It makes a shape (you have none) in a space
It gives perspective to. You sink in it
And disappear there, foundered without trace.

And dreadful alienations bring you down
Into a proper loneliness. You cry
For limits that make a wildcat possible
And laws that tumble ravens in the sky.

—Till clenched hand opens, drowning into you,
Where mackerel, wildcat, raven never fall
Out of their proper spaces; and you are
Perpetual resurrection of them all.

NO CHOICE

I think about you
in as many ways as rain comes.

(I am growing, as I get older,
to hate metaphors—their exactness
and their inadequacy.)

Sometimes these thoughts are
a moistness, hardly falling, than which
nothing is more gentle:
sometimes, a rattling shower, a
bustling Spring-cleaning of the mind:
sometimes, a drowning downpour.

I am growing, as I get older,
to hate metaphor,
to love gentleness,
to fear downpours.

SO MANY WORLDS

I stand for a few minutes
at the mouth of Hell's Glen.
Not because I think there are devils in it
and generations of the dead
being tortured for the sins they can't forget.

Behind me the loch I know so well
smiles in the sun and laughs along its shores.
It's part of my Paradise—
and not a saint in it
nor harps twangling
their endless tunes.

Always between two worlds,
Hell's Glen and Paradise—
where the moon brushes its way
through groves of birch trees
and ice floes ignore those silent dancers
in the midnight sky
and cities that have died
send their ghosts
into the streets of Edinburgh
and the words she spoke changed my darkness
into a summer morning, friendly as a fireside.

MEMORIAL

Everywhere she dies. Everywhere I go she dies.
No sunrise, no city square, no lurking beautiful mountain
but has her death in it.
The silence of her dying sounds through
the carousel of language, it's a web
on which laughter stitches itself. How can my hand
clasp another's when between them
is that thick death, that intolerable distance?

She grieves for my grief. Dying, she tells me
that bird dives from the sun, that fish
leaps into it. No crocus is carved more gently
than the way her dying
shapes my mind.—But I hear, too,
the other words,
black words that make the sound
of soundlessness, that name the nowhere
she is continuously going into.

Ever since she died
she can't stop dying. She makes me
her elegy. I am a walking masterpiece,
a true fiction
of the ugliness of death.
I am her sad music.

INCIDENT

I look across the table and think
(fiery with love)
Ask me, go on, ask me
to do something impossible,
something freakishly useless,
something unimaginable and inimitable
like making a finger break into blossom
or walking for half an hour in twenty minutes
or remembering tomorrow.

I will you to ask it.
But all you say is
Will you give me a cigarette, please?
And I smile and,
returning to the marvellous world
of possibility,
I give you one
with a hand that trembles
with a human trembling.

NOTATIONS OF TEN SUMMER MINUTES

A boy skips flat stones out to sea—each does fine
till a small wave meets it head on and swallows it.
The boy will do the same.

The schoolmaster stands looking out of the window
with one Latin eye and one Greek one.
A boat rounds the point in Gaelic.

Out of the shop comes a stream
of Omo, Weetabix, BiSoDol tablets and a man
with a pocket shaped like a whisky bottle.

Lord V. walks by with the village in his pocket.
Angus walks by
spending the village into the air.

A melodeon is wheezing a clear-throated jig
on the deck of the *Arcadia*. On the shore hills Pan
cocks a hairy ear; and falls asleep again.

The ten minutes are up, except they aren't.
I leave the village, except I don't.
The jig fades to silence, except it doesn't.

WATER TAP

There was this hayfield,
You remember, pale gold
If it weren't hazed
With a million clover heads.

A rope of water
Frayed down—the bucket
Hoisted up a plate
Of flashing light.

The thin road screwed
Into hills; all ended
Journeys were somewhere,
But far, far.

You laughed, by the fence;
And everything that was
Hoisting water
Suddenly spilled over.

—

Edwin Morgan

—

BORN IN GLASGOW in 1920, Edwin Morgan was educated at Rutherglen Academy and Glasgow High School. After first considering Art School he started a degree in English literature at Glasgow University. His studies were interrupted in 1940 by the war and he spent the next six years with the Royal Army Medical Corps, serving in Egypt, Palestine and the Lebanon as part of the North African Campaign. Morgan returned to Scotland and finished his degree in 1947, turning down the chance to go to Oxford in order to remain at Glasgow. He joined the English Department at the University and worked there as a lecturer and a distinguished literary critic for over thirty years, becoming Titular Professor in 1975. He is now Professor Emeritus at Glasgow and a visiting Professor at the University of Strathclyde.

As an internationally respected translator, Edwin Morgan received the Soros translation award in New York in 1985. He has written a study of Eastern European poets and translated verse by Montale, Brecht, Neruda, Pasternak, Yevtushenko, Martynov, Tsvetayeva, Weöres and Juhász, not to mention *Beowulf* into modern English and Mayakovsky into Scots. His critical work includes a study of Hugh MacDiarmid and two collections of essays, including a number of key articles on the role of the poet in modern culture which, as always, demonstrate the resolutely international outlook which has taken him all over the world on lecture tours, visits and poetry readings. Edwin Morgan's many volumes of poems began with *The Vision of Cathkin Braes* in 1952, while 1990 saw his seventieth birthday and a special edition of his *Collected Poems*.

More than any other contemporary poet in English, Edwin Morgan has set out to come to terms with how science, technology and new methods of communication are changing our world and how we see it. He has written many concrete poems as well as 'science fiction' poems such as 'From the Domain of Arnheim', and poems based on the conceptual and expressive properties of imagined newspaper snapshots (the *Instamatic Poems*) and video-taping, as in *From the Video Box*. Such work welcomes the fluidity of the modern world, and although he is not blind to its dreadful aspects, Morgan has always been optimistic about the capacity of the human spirit to change, to endure and to thrive.

Morgan comes closer to home with the many poems he has written about cities in general and Glasgow in particular. Works such as 'The Second Life', 'The Woman', 'Trio', 'In the Snack-bar', 'Christmas Eve' and 'For Bonfires' reveal him as one of our finest modern poets of the urban experience. In these poems, as in his love lyrics ('One Cigarette', 'Absence', 'Fado'), Edwin Morgan writes with great poignancy about the fleeting nature of personal contact amid the rush of crowds and the sea of information which is where we live. From this territory he has written very fine lyrics of solitude, beauty and desolation, and yet his delight in astonishment, balance and (always) regeneration makes 'Cinquevalli' something of a personal statement for him, and shines through 'Instructions to an Actor'.

But does every man feel like this at forty—
I mean it's like Thomas Wolfe's New York, his
heady light, the stunning plunging canyons, beauty—
pale stars winking hazy downtown quitting-time,
and the winter moon flooding the skyscrapers, northern—
an aspiring place, glory of the bridges, foghorns
are enormous messages, a looming mastery
that lays its hand on the young man's bowels
until he feels in that air, that rising spirit
all things are possible, he rises with it
until he feels that he can never die—
Can it be like this, and is this what it means
in Glasgow now, writing as the aircraft roar
over building sites, in this warm west light
by the daffodil banks that were never so crowded and lavish—
green May, and the slow great blocks rising
under yellow tower cranes, concrete and glass and steel
out of a dour rubble it was and barefoot children gone—
Is it only the slow stirring, a city's renewed life
that stirs me, could it stir me so deeply
as May, but could May have stirred
what I feel of desire and strength
like an arm saluting a sun?

All January, all February the skaters
enjoyed Bingham's pond, the crisp cold evenings,
they swung and flashed among car headlights,
the drivers parked round the unlit pond
to watch them, and give them light, what laughter
and pleasure rose in the rare lulls
of the yards-away stream of wheels along Great Western Road!
The ice broke up, but the boats came out.

The painted boats are ready for pleasure.
The long light needs no headlamps.

Black oar cuts a glitter: it is heaven on earth.

Is it true that we come alive
not once, but many times?
We are drawn back to the image
of the seed in darkness, or the greying skin
of the snake that hides a shining one—
it will push that used-up matter off
and even the film of the eye is sloughed—
That the world may be the same, and we are not
and so the world is not the same,
the second eye is making again
this place, these waters and these towers,
they are rising again
as the eye stands up to the sun,
as the eye salutes the sun.

Many things are unspoken
in the life of a man, and with a place
there is an unspoken love also
in undercurrents, drifting, waiting its time.
A great place and its people are not renewed lightly.
The caked layers of grime
grow warm, like homely coats.
But yet they will be dislodged
and men will still be warm.
The old coats are discarded.
The old ice is loosed.
The old seeds are awake

Slip out of darkness, it is time.

ONE CIGARETTE

No smoke without you, my fire.
After you left,
your cigarette glowed on in my ashtray
and sent up a long thread of such quiet grey
I smiled to wonder who would believe its signal
of so much love. One cigarette
in the non-smoker's tray.
As the last spire
trembles up, a sudden draught
blows it winding into my face.
Is it smell, is it taste?
You are here again, and I am drunk on your tobacco lips.
Out with the light.
Let the smoke lie back in the dark.
Till I hear the very ash
sigh down among the flowers of brass
I'll breathe, and long past midnight, your last kiss.

ABSENCE

My shadow—
I woke to a wind swirling the curtains light and dark
and the birds twittering on the roofs, I lay cold
in the early light in my room high over London.
What fear was it that made the wind sound like a fire
so that I got up and looked out half-asleep
at the calm rows of street-lights fading far below?
Without fire
only the wind blew.
But in the dream I woke from, you
came running through the traffic, tugging me, clinging
to my elbow, your eyes spoke
what I could not grasp—
Nothing, if you were here!

The wind of the early quiet
merges slowly now with a thousand rolling wheels.
The lights are out, the air is loud.
It is an ordinary January day.
My shadow, do you hear the streets?
Are you at my heels? Are you here?
And I throw back the sheets.

THE WOMAN

A string of pearls
in the dark window, that wet spring,
sometimes a white hand raised with a cigarette
blurred by rain and buses
anyhow. A lonely
ring.

Nothing she was waiting for
came, unless what took her
in the coldest arms.

It seems to be the pearls
we remember, for what they spoke
of another life than waiting,
and being unknown dying
in a high dark street.

Who she was you'll keep thinking.
The hearse rolled off in thunder,
but showers only lay dust.

FROM THE DOMAIN OF ARNHEIM*

And so that all these ages, these years
we cast behind us, like the smoke-clouds
dragged back into vacancy when the rocket springs—

The domain of Arnheim was all snow, but we were there.
We saw a yellow light thrown on the icefield
from the huts by the pines, and laughter came up
floating from a white corrie
miles away, clearly.
We moved on down, arm in arm.
I know you would have thought it was a dream
but we were there. And those were trumpets—
tremendous round the rocks—
while they were burning fires of trash and mammoths' bones.
They sang naked, and kissed in the smoke.
A child, or one of their animals, was crying.
Young men blew the ice crystals off their drums.
We came down among them, but of course
they could see nothing, on their time-scale.
Yet they sensed us, stopped, looked up—even into our eyes.
To them we were a displacement of the air,
a sudden chill, yet we had no power
over their fear. If one of them had been dying
he would have died. The crying
came from one just born: that was the cause
of the song. We saw it now. What had we stopped
but joy?
I know you felt
the same dismay, you gripped my arm, they were waiting
for what they knew of us to pass.
A sweating trumpeter took
a brand from the fire with a shout and threw it

where our bodies would have been—
we felt nothing but his courage.
And so they would deal with every imagined power
seen or unseen.
There are no gods in the domain of Arnheim.

We signalled to the ship; got back;
our lives and days returned to us, but
haunted by deeper souvenirs than any rocks or seeds.
From time the souvenirs are deeds.

*Arnheim: a mysterious realm in a story by Edgar Allan Poe. 'The
Domain of Arnheim' is the title of a haunting mountainscape by
the surrealist painter René Magritte.

FADO

Fold those waves away
and take the yellow, yellow bay,
roll it up like Saturday.

No use the sleepy sand,
no use my breasts in his brown hand.
I danced on tables in that land.

Grim is my cold sun.
Through my street the long rains run.
Thousands I see, thinking of one.

WINTER*

The year goes, the woods decay, and after,
many a summer dies. The swan
on Bingham's pond, a ghost, comes and goes.
It goes, and ice appears, it holds,
bears gulls that stand around surprised,
blinking in the heavy light, bears boys
when skates take over swan-tracks gone.
After many summer dyes, the swan-white ice
glints only crystal beyond white. Even
dearest blue's not there, though poets would find it.
I find one stark scene
cut by evening cries, by warring air.
The muffled hiss of blades escapes into breath,
hangs with it a moment, fades off.
Fades off, goes, the scene, the voices fade,
the line of trees, the woods that fall, decay
and break, the dark comes down, the shouts
run off into it and disappear.
At last the lamps go too, when fog
drives monstrous down the dual carriageway
out to the west, and even in my room
and on this paper I do not know
about that grey dead pane
of ice that sees nothing and that nothing sees.

*This poem contains lines and echoes from the opening of
Tennyson's 'Tithonus'.

John S. Clarke,* festooned with snakes, said, 'Touch one,
look closely, they're quite beautiful; not slimy;
come on, come down to the front now, that's better.
Don't be afraid, girls, aren't these eyes pure jewels?
Come on lads, stretch your hands out, try this johnny,
I bet it's like no creature you ever handled.'
I thought the lecture had been good, but this was
unforeseen, an unknown world, strange bonus—
the dry brown coil was at first almost leaden,
slightly rough but inert, with scales tight-fitting
like Inca walls, till what seemed a faint tickling
became a very crawling of the flesh as
movement began to test my arm, the ripples
of an almost unfathomable power
rhythmically saying, I am living:
you may not love me but oh how I am living!
And it is all one life, in tanks, bags, boxes,
lecture-theatres, outhouses, fronds of bracken,
rivers for men and serpents to swim over
from dark bank to dark bank and vanish quickly
about their business in raw grass and reedland,
scale, sole, palm, tail, brow, roving, brushing, touching.

*Socialist educator and popular speaker on science and knowledge
in Glasgow in the 1930s.

THE APPLE'S SONG

Tap me with your finger,
rub me with your sleeve,
hold me, sniff me, peel me
curling round and round
till I burst out white and cold
from my tight red coat
and tingle in your palm
as if I'd melt and breathe
a living pomander
waiting for the minute
of joy when you lift me
to your mouth and crush me
and in taste and fragrance
I race through your head
in my dizzy dissolve.

I sit in the bowl
in my cool corner
and watch you as you pass
smoothing your apron.
Are you thirsty yet?
My eyes are shining.

HYENA

I am waiting for you.
I have been travelling all morning through the bush
and not eaten.
I am lying at the edge of the bush
on a dusty path that leads from the burnt-out kraal.
I am panting, it is midday, I found no water-hole.
I am very fierce without food and although my eyes
are screwed to slits against the sun
you must believe I am prepared to spring.

What do you think of me?
I have a rough coat like Africa.
I am crafty with dark spots
like the bush-tufted plains of Africa.
I sprawl as a shaggy bundle of gathered energy
like Africa sprawling in its waters.
I trot, I lope, I slaver, I am a ranger.
I hunch my shoulders. I eat the dead.

Do you like my song?
When the moon pours hard and cold on the veldt
I sing, and I am the slave of darkness.
Over the stone walls and the mud walls and the ruined places
and the owls, the moonlight falls.
I sniff a broken drum. I bristle. My pelt is silver.
I howl my song to the moon—up it goes.
Would you meet me there in the waste places?

It is said I am a good match
for a dead lion. I put my muzzle
at his golden flanks, and tear. He
is my golden supper, but my tastes are easy.

I have a crowd of fangs, and I use them.
Oh and my tongue—do you like me
when it comes lolling out over my jaw
very long, and I am laughing?
I am not laughing.
But I am not snarling either, only
panting in the sun, showing you
what I grip
carrion with.

I am waiting
for the foot to slide,
for the heart to seize,
for the leaping sinews to go slack,
for the fight to the death to be fought to the death,
for a glazing eye and the rumour of blood.
I am crouching in my dry shadows
till you are ready for me.
My place is to pick you clean
and leave your bones to the wind.

THE MUMMY

(The Mummy [of Rameses II] *was met at Orly airport by Mme Saunier-Seïté.*—News item, Sept. 1976)

—May I welcome Your Majesty to Paris.

—Mm.

—I hope the flight from Cairo was reasonable.

—Mmmmm.

—We have a germ-proof room at the Museum of Man
  where we trust Your Majesty will have peace and quiet.

—Unh-unh.

—I am sorry, but this is necessary.
  Your Majesty's person harbours a fungus.

—Fng fng's, hn?

—Well, it is something attacking your cells.
  Your Majesty is gently deteriorating
  after nearly four thousand years
  becalmed in masterly embalmment.
  We wish to save you from the worm.

—Wrm hrm! Mgh-mgh-mgh.

—Indeed I know it must be distressing
  to a pharaoh and a son of Ra,
  to the excavator of Abu Simbel

that glorious temple in the rock,
to the perfecter of Karnak hall,
to the hammer of the Hittites,
to the colossus whose colossus
raised in red granite at holy Thebes
sixteen-men-high astounds the desert
shattered, as Your Majesty in life
shattered the kingdom and oppressed the poor
with such lavish grandeur and panache,
to Rameses, to Ozymandias,
to the Louis Quatorze of the Nile,
how bitter it must be to feel
a microbe eat your camphored bands.
But we are here to help Your Majesty.
We shall encourage you to unwind.
You have many useful years ahead.

—M' n'm 'z 'zym'ndias, kng'v kngz!

—Yes yes. Well, Shelley is dead now.
He was not embalmed. He will not write
about Your Majesty again.

—T't'nkh'm'n? H'tsh'ps't?
'khn't'n? N'f' rt'ti? Mm? Mm?

—The hall of fame has many mansions.
You Majesty may rest assured
your deeds will always be remembered.

—Youmm w'm'nn. B't'f'lll w'm'nnnn.
No w'm'nnn f'r th'zndz y'rz.

—Your Majesty, what are you doing?

—Ng! Mm. Mhm. Mm? Mm? Mmmmm.

—Your Majesty, Your Majesty! You'll break your
stitches!

—Fng st'chez fng's wrm hrm.

—I really hate to have to use
  a hypodermic on a mummy,
  but we cannot have you strain yourself.
  Remember your fungus, Your Majesty.

—Fng. Zzzzzzz.

—That's right.

—Aaaaaaaaah.

CONSTRUCTION FOR I.K. BRUNEL

I AM BARD   DOM BRUMEL
I AM ISOBAR   DOM BOOMMILL
I AM IRON BAR   DOM BROODWELL
I AM IRON BARD   DOM BREWMETAL
I AM BY ASGARD   DOM BROOKMEDDLE
I AM IRON ICEBERG great western suspension steam telegraph king   DOM BRUNELLESCHAL
I STAND GUARD   great eastern hungerford canal cableboat king   DOM BLOOMMIDDLE
I SPAN BARRED   great clifton railtunnel docks submarine king   DOM BLUEMEZZO
I SEEM BARED   great britain explosions locks towerpier king   DOM BOONMEDAL
I STAB HARD   DOM BRUMMELL

· 65 ·

A cup capsizes along the formica,
slithering with a dull clatter.
A few heads turn in the crowded evening snack-bar.
An old man is trying to get to his feet
from the low round stool fixed to the floor.
Slowly he levers himself up, his hands have no power.
He is up as far as he can get. The dismal hump
looming over him forces his head down.
He stands in his stained beltless gaberdine
like a monstrous animal caught in a tent
in some story. He sways slightly,
the face not seen, bent down
in shadow under his cap.
Even on his feet he is staring at the floor
or would be, if he could see.
I notice now his stick, once painted white
but scuffed and muddy, hanging from his right arm.
Long blind, hunchback born, half paralysed
he stands
fumbling with the stick
and speaks:
'I want—to go to the—toilet.'

It is down two flights of stairs, but we go.
I take his arm. 'Give me—your arm—it's better,' he says.
Inch by inch we drift towards the stairs.
A few yards of floor are like a landscape
to be negotiated, in the slow setting out
time has almost stopped. I concentrate
my life to his: crunch of spilt sugar,
slidy puddle from the night's umbrellas,
table edges, people's feet,

hiss of the coffee-machine, voices and laughter,
smell of a cigar, hamburgers, wet coats steaming,
and the slow dangerous inches to the stairs.
I put his right hand on the rail
and take his stick. He clings to me. The stick
is in his left hand, probing the treads.
I guide his arm and tell him the steps.
And slowly we go down. And slowly we go down.
White tiles and mirrors at last. He shambles
uncouth into the clinical gleam.
I set him in position, stand behind him
and wait with his stick.
His brooding reflection darkens the mirror
but the trickle of his water is thin and slow,
an old man's apology for living.
Painful ages to close his trousers and coat—
I do up the last buttons for him.
He asks doubtfully, 'Can I—wash my hands?'
I fill the basin, clasp his soft fingers round the soap.
He washes, feebly, patiently. There is no towel.
I press the pedal of the drier, draw his hands
gently into the roar of the hot air.
But he cannot rub them together,
drags out a handkerchief to finish.
He is glad to leave the contraption, and face the stairs.
He climbs, and steadily enough.
He climbs, we climb. He climbs
with many pauses but with that one
persisting patience of the undefeated
which is the nature of man when all is said.
And slowly we go up. And slowly we go up.
The faltering, unfaltering steps
take him at last to the door
across that endless, yet not endless waste of floor.

I watch him helped on a bus. It shudders off in the rain.
The conductor bends to hear where he wants to go.

Wherever he could go it would be dark
and yet he must trust men.
Without embarrassment or shame
he must announce his most pitiful needs
in a public place. No one sees his face.
Does he know how frightening he is in his strangeness
under his mountainous coat, his hands like wet leaves
stuck to the half-white stick?
His life depends on many who would evade him.
But he cannot reckon up the chances,
having one thing to do,
to haul his blind hump through these rains of August.
Dear Christ, to be born for this!

TRIO

Coming up Buchanan Street, quickly, on a sharp winter evening
a young man and two girls, under the Christmas lights—
The young man carries a new guitar in his arms,
the girl on the inside carries a very young baby,
and the girl on the outside carries a chihuahua.
And the three of them are laughing, their breath rises
in a cloud of happiness, and as they pass
the boy says, 'Wait till he sees this but!'
The chihuahua has a tiny Royal Stewart tartan coat like a teapot-
    holder,
the baby in its white shawl is all bright eyes and mouth like favours
    in a fresh sweet cake,
the guitar swells out under its milky plastic cover, tied at the neck
    with silver tinsel tape and a brisk sprig of mistletoe.
Orphean sprig! Melting baby! Warm chihuahua!
The vale of tears is powerless before you.
Whether Christ is born, or is not born, you
put paid to fate, it abdicates
                            under the Christmas lights.
Monsters of the year
go blank, are scattered back,
can't bear this march of three.

— And the three have passed, vanished in the crowd
(yet not vanished, for in their arms they wind
the life of men and beasts, and music,
laughter ringing them round like a guard)
at the end of this winter's day.

CHRISTMAS EVE

Loneliness of city Christmas Eves—
with real stars up there—clear—and stars
on poles and wires across the street, and streaming
cars all dark with parcels, home
to families and the lighted window trees—

I sat down in the bus beside him—white jeans,
black jerkin, slumped with head nodding
in sleep, face hidden by long black hair, hands
tattooed on the four fingers ADEN 1967
and on the right hand five Christian crosses.
As the bus jerked, his hand fell on my knee,
stayed there, lay heavily and alive
with blue carvings from another world
and seemed to hold me like a claw,
unmoving. It moved. I rubbed my ear
to steal a glance at him, found him
stealing a glance at me. It was not
the jerking of the bus, it was a proposition.
He shook his hair back, and I saw his face
for the first time, unshaven, hardman, a warning
whether in Aden or Glasgow, but our eyes held
while that blue hand burned into my leg.
Half drunk, half sleeping—but half what, half what?
As his hand stirred again, my arm covered it
while the bus jolted round a corner.
'Don't ge' aff tae ah ge' aff.'—But the conductor
was watching, came up and shook him, looked at me.
My ticket was up, I had to leave him sprawled there
with that hand that now seemed so defenceless
lying on the seat I had left. Half down the stair

I looked back. The last thing I saw was Aden
and five blue crosses for five dead friends.

It was only fifteen minutes out of life
but I feel as if I was lifted by a whirlwind
and thrown down on some desert rocks to die
of dangers as always far worse lost than run.

FOR BONFIRES

The leaves are gathered, the trees are dying
for a time.
A seagull cries through white smoke in the garden fires
that fill the heavy air.
All day heavy air
is burning, a moody dog
sniffs and circles the swish of the rake.
In streaks of ash, the gardener drifting
ghostly, beats his hands, a cloud
of breath to the red sun.

II

An island in the city, happy demolition men
behind windowed hoardings—look at them
trailing drills through rubble dust, kicking rubble,
smoking leaning on a pick, putting the stub
over an ear and the hot yellow helmet over that,
whistling up the collapsing chimney, kicking the
ricochet, rattling the trail with
snakes of wire, slamming slabs
down, plaster, cornice, brick, brick
on broken brick and plaster dust,
sprawling with steaming cans and pieces
at noon, afternoon bare sweat shining
paths down chalky backs, coughing
in filtered sunshine, slithering, swearing,
joking, slowly stacking and building
their rubbish into a total bonfire.
Look at that Irishman, bending
in a beautiful arc to throw
the last black rafter to the top,

stands back, walks round it singing
as it crackles into flame—old doors,
old beams, boxes, window-frames,
a rag doll, sacks, flex, old newspapers,
burst shelves, a shoe, old dusters, rags of
wallpaper roses. And they all stand round,
and cheer the tenement to smoke

III
In a galvanized bucket
the letters burn. They roar and twist
and the leaves curl back one by one.
They put out claws and scrape the iron
like a living thing,
but the scrabbling to be free soon subsides.
The black pages fuse
to a single whispering mass
threaded by dying tracks of gold.
Let them grow cold,
and when they're dead
quickly draw breath.

From *Instamatic Poems**

VENICE APRIL 1971

Three black gondolas
cut the sparkle of the lagoon.

In the first, the Greek archimandrite
stands, a young black-bearded man
in gold cope, black hood, black shoulder veil blown back
in the sunny breeze. In front of him
his even younger acolyte holds high
the glittering processional cross. His long black robe
glitters with delicious silver flowers
against the blue of the sky.

In the second gondola Stravinsky goes.
The black fringe trails the lapping water,
the heavy coffin dips the golden lions on the sides,
the gondoliers are ankle-deep in roses,
the coffin sways crowned with roses,
the gondoliers' white blouses and black sashes
startle their brown arms, the shining oars,
the pink and crimson flowers.

And the third gondola
is like a shadow
where the widow goes.

And there at the edge of the picture
where the crowds cross themselves
and weep a little in the Italian way,
an old poet with white hair†
and hooded, piercing eyes

leans on his stick
and without expression
watches the boats move out
from his shore.

*The *Instamatic Poems* are imagined 'snapshots' based on stories
reported in the world's daily news.
†Exiled from America, Ezra Pound was living an isolated life in
Venice. He died the following year.

An American skindiver's shot, inside the wreck
of one of the largest Japanese submarines,
the Shinohara, sunk in '44.
A coral plug fills the hatch
of the engine room; brass gauges
blink through the brown sediment
of twenty-seven years; a row of femurs
rests on the ledge of the starboard engine.
In the flash, the silt of the floor stirs faintly
but everything is very still. Bones shine
half out of silt, or
from a glove of coral, or
lie crossed like cuneiform
too hard to decipher on tablets of sand.
Nothing wavers, the Pacific
is at peace under Truk.
Only the living jet of bubbles from the diver
has loosened off a flake of rust
which hangs, perfectly suspended
in the tomb of the victor's strobe.

7

It is hard to know what it is I saw.
I had been switching through a score of channels
in that disgruntled and half-idle mood I'm sure you know,
a gloomy winter's evening with the curtains open,
the streetlamps on and the cars racing home,
and gusts of wind that shook the house,
raced off with armfuls of showers to the river.
Who can be happy? Not I. But the search
goes on, even through that flurry of switched images,
as if a picture, if at least it moved, could move
the sluggish heart. Everything happens, perhaps.
There was suddenly something growing on the screen
that could kick-start hope racing forward
into I don't know what roads of years.
There were no images, that's the hardest part.
The whole screen was a swirling dirty grey
that churned and churned and held the attention
only to wonder what it was; but there in the middle
it seemed to split like a skin, a thin
horizontal streak of blue flashed out—
no, it did not flash, that was only the surprise
of the contrast, it was too pure a blue,
an eggshell blue, a sky blue, blue
of an innocent eye, not harsh or icy,
not brooding dark or royal,
not feeble pastel either,
but clear and steady, beautiful and true.
It grew, like a rift in the clouds after rain,
or like the slow opening of an eye,
until the grey clouds, the grey lids, gathered
their hideous strength and grain by grain

joined seamlessly together once again.
Wherever I go I see that patch of blue.
Did anyone else watch it? Is there happiness?
Hope in things that come and go?
Why should we not know?

*The Video Box poems are based on the concept of the video booths in which viewers can record their opinions as shown in Gus MacDonald's 'Right to Reply' programmes for Channel 4.

Cinquevalli is falling, falling.
The shining trapeze kicks and flirts free,
solo performer at last.
The sawdust puffs up with a thump,
settles on a tangle of broken limbs.
St Petersburg screams and leans.
His pulse flickers with the gas-jets. He lives.

Cinquevalli has a therapy.
In his hospital bed, in his hospital chair
he holds a ball, lightly, lets it roll round his hand,
or grips it tight, gauging its weight and resistance,
begins to balance it, to feel its life attached to his
by will and knowledge, invisible strings
that only he can see. He throws it
from hand to hand, always different,
always the same, always
different, always the
same.
His muscles learn to think, his arms grow very strong.

Cinquevalli in sepia
looks at me from an old postcard: bundle of enigmas.
Half faun, half military man; almond eyes, curly hair,
conventional moustache; tights, and a tunic loaded
with embroideries, tassels, chains, fringes; hand on hip
with a large signet-ring winking at the camera
but a bull neck and shoulders and a cannon-ball
at his elbow as he stands by the posing pedestal;
half reluctant, half truculent,
half handsome, half absurd,
but let me see you forget him: not to be done.

Cinquevalli is a juggler.
In a thousand theatres, in every continent,
he is the best, the greatest. After eight years perfecting
he can balance one billiard ball on another billiard ball
on top of a cue on top of a third billiard ball
in a wine-glass held in his mouth. To those
who say the balls are waxed, or flattened,
he patiently explains the trick will only work
because the spheres are absolutely true.
There is no deception in him. He is true.

Cinquevalli is juggling with a bowler,
a walking-stick, a cigar, and a coin.
Who foresees? How to please.
The last time round, the bowler
flies to his head, the stick sticks in his hand,
the cigar jumps into his mouth, the coin
lands on his foot—ah, but
is kicked into his eye
and held there as the miraculous monocle
without which the portrait would be incomplete.

Cinquevalli is practising.
He sits in his dressing-room talking to some friends,
at the same time writing a letter with one hand
and with the other juggling four balls.
His friends think of demons, but
'You could all do this,' he says,
sealing the letter with a billiard ball.

Cinquevalli is on the high wire in Odessa.
The roof cracks, he is falling, falling
into the audience, a woman breaks his fall,
he cracks her like a flea, but lives.

Cinquevalli broods in his armchair in Brixton Road.
He reads in the paper about the shells whining
at Passchendaele, imagines the mud and the dead.
He goes to the window and wonders through that dark evening
what is happening in Poland where he was born.
His neighbours call him a German spy.
'Kestner, Paul Kestner, that's his name!'
'Keep Kestner out of the British music-hall!'
He frowns; it is cold; his fingers seem stiff and old.

Cinquevalli tosses up a plate of soup
and twirls it on his forefinger; not a drop spills.
He laughs, and well may he laugh
who can do that. The astonished table
breathe again, laugh too, think the world
a spinning thing that spills, for a moment, no drop.

Cinquevalli's coffin sways through Brixton
only a few months before the Armistice.
Like some trick they cannot get off the ground
it seems to burden the shuffling bearers, all their arms
cross-juggle that displaced person, that man
of balance, of strength, of delights and marvels,
in his unsteady box at last into the earth.

INSTRUCTIONS TO AN ACTOR*

Now, boy, remember this is the great scene.
You'll stand on a pedestal behind a curtain,
the curtain will be drawn, and then you don't move
for eighty lines; don't move, don't speak, don't breathe.
I'll stun them all out there, I'll scare them,
make them weep, but it depends on you.
I warn you eighty lines is a long time,
but you don't breathe, you're dead,
you're a dead queen, a statue,
you're dead as stone, new-carved,
new-painted and the paint not dry
—we'll get some red to keep your lip shining—
and you're a mature woman, you've got dignity,
some beauty still in middle age, and
you're kind and true, but you're dead,
your husband thinks you're dead,
the audience thinks you're dead,
and you don't breathe, boy, I say
you don't even blink for eighty lines,
if you blink you're out!
Fix your eye on something and keep watching it.
Practise when you get home. It can be done.
And you move at last—music's the cue.
When you hear a mysterious solemn jangle
of instruments, make yourself ready.
Five lines more, you can lift a hand.
It may tingle a bit, but lift it—
slow, slow—
O this is where I hit them
right between the eyes, I've got them now—
I'm making the dead walk—
you move a foot, slow, steady, down,

you guard your balance in case you're stiff,
you move, you step down, down from the pedestal,
control your skirt with one hand, the other hand
you now hold out—
O this will melt their hearts if nothing does—
to your husband who wronged you long ago
and hesitates in amazement
to believe you are alive.
Finally he embraces you, and there's nothing
I can give you to say, boy,
but you must show that you have forgiven him.
Forgiveness, that's the thing. It's like a second life.
I know you can do it.—Right then, shall we try?

*The reconciliation scene at the close of Shakespeare's *The Winter's Tale* in which the statue of Hermione comes alive to return to the arms of her husband King Leontes.

REVOLVING RESTAURANT

As round we go, round we go,
not like that but very slow,
we watch the whole Bay far below.

The lifted fork stands still to scan
that best of twilights made by man,
enchanted metropolitan.

The lights come on, the dark comes down,
gold winks through tufts of leafy brown,
mist-grey waters lap the town.

Bridges, banks, hotels are creeping,
brilliant, silently unsleeping,
in and out of our rapt keeping.

Look, is that London?—Not that one,
no city, but one beyond the sun—
Jack—in his boat—when day is done—

sailing well out to make a catch
beneath the stars? We'll never match
him, toying with our harmless batch

of sprouts, to muzak, or the sea
where only thoughts, wishes, can be
as round we go, and think us free.

—

Liz Lochhead

—

BORN IN 1947 and educated in Motherwell, Liz Lochhead went to Glasgow School of Art in 1965. After graduating in 1970 she worked as a teacher for several years before becoming a full-time writer in 1978. She has written a number of plays and works for the stage, including an exploration of Mary Shelley and the mythology of the Frankenstein monster in *Blood and Ice*, a historical play in modern idiom, *Mary Queen of Scots Got Her Head Chopped Off*, as well as *Same Difference, Dracula, The Big Picture* and *Them Through the Wall* (with Agnes Owen). She has done a Scots translation of Molière's *Tartuffe*, plays for radio and television, and many sketches, raps and performance pieces for reviews in Edinburgh, Glasgow and on tour. She has held a number of writing fellowships as well as being writer in residence at the Royal Shakespeare Company. A familiar and popular performer on radio, television and live readings around the country and abroad, Liz Lochhead's comic and satirical verses and songs were published as *True Confessions and New Clichés* where a number of her brilliant monologues ('Verena: Security') can also be found.

Lochhead's first book of poems was *Memo for Spring* (1972), followed by *Islands* (1978) and *The Grim Sisters* (1981), while *Dreaming Frankenstein* (1984) contained all her previous work and new poems as well. Her most recent collection is *Bagpipe Muzak* (1991).

Liz Lochhead's 'Outer' poems show her responses to the life and landscape of the Outer Hebrides, but her particular strength as a writer comes from an edgy and alert eye for personal relationships especially when an element of sexual tension is present ('Box Room','Midsummer Night', 'Stooge Song'). She delights in puns and the tacky paraphernalia of the commercial world, with its 'new improved' formulae, but poems such as 'The Grim Sisters' and 'The Empty Song' also use this unlikely material to achieve a poignant eloquence at the plight of women in the face of such idealised and unrealisable images. 'Fourth of July Fireworks' casts the same sensitive and nervous awareness on American society and the poet's status there as a (visiting) outsider, while 'Hafiz on Danforth Avenue' gives the same edge to a more personal poem constructed from images in memory and the random babble and blur of street life around her. By comparison 'Mirror's Song' and 'The Other Woman' are much darker poems in which the dialogue with another has become an inner dialogue with some second self— a female persona given over to 'permanents and panstick and / Coty'. There is an extraordinary force to these pieces as the poet confronts nothing less than terror and rage on the other side of the mirror which symbolizes the entrapment of stereotyped femininity, the puzzle of identity, and the liberating force of her art.

BOX ROOM

First the welcoming. Smiles all round. A space
For handshakes. Then she put me in my place—
(Oh, with concern for my comfort). 'This room
Was always his—when he comes home
It's here for him. Unless of course,' she said,
'He brings a Friend.' She smiled 'I hope the bed
Is soft enough? He'll make do tonight
In the lounge on the put-u-up. All right
For a night or two. Once or twice before
He's slept there. It'll all be fine I'm sure—
Next door if you want to wash your face.'
Leaving me 'peace to unpack' she goes. My weekend case
(Lightweight, glossy, made of some synthetic
Miracle) and I are left alone in her pathetic
Shrine to your lost boyhood. She must
Think she can brush off time with dust
From model aeroplanes. I laugh it off in self defence,
Who have come for a weekend to state my permanence.

Peace to unpack—but I found none
In this spare room which once contained you. (Dun-
Coloured walls, one small window which used to frame
Your old horizons). What can I blame
For my unrest, insomnia? Persistent fear
Elbows me, embedded deeply here
In an outgrown bed. (Narrow, but no narrower
Than the single bed we sometimes share).
On every side you grin gilt edged from long-discarded selves
(But where do I fit into the picture?) Your bookshelves
Are crowded with previous prizes, a selection
Of plots grown thin. Your egg collection
Shatters me—that now you have no interest

In.(You just took one from each, you never wrecked a nest,
You said).Invited guest among abandoned objects, my position
Is precarious, closeted so—it's dark, your past a premonition
I can't close my eyes to. I shiver despite
The electric blanket and the deceptive mildness of the night.

From *Islands*

OUTER: 1

Another life
we marvel at the tweeds
a bale by each gatepost.
This is the day the lorry will collect
granite-marl   green-lovatt
herringbone   houndstooth   rust and
heathermix.

From each dour house
always this always black
and white dog comes to stand stock still.
He's only ruffled by the wind.
He doesn't waste a bark. He's only
here to check we skirt his land.

Another life
each spare rib croft
each staggered drystane wall
that makes slicing up bare land
look next to natural.
Low houses   separate   strung across the hill
so far away from us—
the woman on the doorstep with a basin
that might be henmash
or monday washing
the man
shut in with the bare bulb
and the clattering in the blacktarred hut
where the weaving gets done

Lambs home in
two hard tugs

and they fasten onto each vague mother.
Absentmindedly it seems
sheep tug at the roots of everything
till it's all baldness stones and droppings.
Hens scratch and pick.
The flagrant cockerel's let crow
from the boss-eyed skull of a rusted truck.
Bones, blackhouses, implements.

Things fall to bits.
Sheep come apart in handfuls—
it's that time of year—
Old cars in the salt air.
Far too many stones to ever clear.

What's not useful lies and rots.
Useless to say ramshackle
or to call it waste.
Nothing goes and leaves no trace—
just that here's a climate where
it's all meshed over, nettled, part of things
in no time. Absorbable.
Rain and mud and wind
will streak and fritter even this too-blue
plastic feedbag till it blends.

Even the weaving will go to the wall
(the hand-
   loom's finished if this doublewidth comes in)
Shawbost Breger Arnol who'll
make ends meet?

For there's a bare living only
if even the godless can pass Sunday
decently idle in their stocking soles
and never cross the door.

If you use the otterboard to trick the fish
and without your nosey neighbour knowing
fit a motor that will turn your loom.
If you don't get caught.
If you can keep the sheep out
your patch might learn a smattering of growth.
Wind combs out wool wraithed
on nebulous necessary fences.

OUTER: V

Golden Harvest.
The Girl Pat.
Eilan Glas.
Naturally sixteen has not much time
for all the old songs.
These two have dogged the Mod
this last afternoon, undone
the top three buttons, folded
collars open to a deep vee—
schoolgirls arm in arm
down by the harbour humming.
Arm in arm
on such high cork shoes they still
move easily
among oil and rope and smeared
rainbows of fishscales.

They giggle
or go blank
or bat back smart answers
to the young dogs (sealegs,
cuffed wellingtons) moving easily
among nets and hooks and weights.

Luminous floats,
wolf whistles.

Trouble is this town's too small.
They've twice trawled round the circuit
of mainstreet and back round church street,
sneered at every white-net Sunday hat with streamers
in the Pakistani draper's shop display.
In the autumn there's the nursing.

At Woolworth's beauty counter
one smears across the back of her hand
the colour of her next kiss.
The other nets in her wiremesh basket
Sea Witch.
Harvest Gold.

OUTER: VI

Laura has gone in a clean white blouse
to Stornaway to sing Beginners Gaelic in the Mod.
Eeshy and Agnes-Mhairi
always laugh she says
and imitate the way incomers talk.
Let them she says.
Living here she wants to learn.
Eleven-years-old,
she'd rather be here than Glasgow anyday.
This is where she wants to stay.
She opens her book. She shines.
We stumble after her, repeat.

Is e seò tigh ban
Is e seò tigh dubh.
This is a white house
This is a black house.

THE BARGAIN

The river in January is fast and high.
You and I
are off to the Barrows.
Gathering police-horses twitch and fret
at the Tron end of London Road and Gallowgate.
The early kick-off we forgot
has us, three-thirty, rubbing the wrong way
against all the ugly losers
getting ready to let fly
where the two rivers meet.

January, and we're
looking back, looking forward,
don't know which way

but the boy
with three beautiful Bakelite
Bush radios for sale in Meadow's minimarket is
buttonpopping stationhopping he
doesn't miss a beat   sings along   it's easy
to every changing tune.

Yes today we're in love aren't we?
with the whole splintering city
its big quick river   wintry bridges
its brazen black Victorian heart.
So what if every other tenement
wears its hearth on its gable end
all I want
is my glad eye to catch
a glint in your flinty Northern face again
just once. Oh I know it's cold

and coming down
and no we never lingered long among
the Shipbank traders.
Paddy's market   underneath the arches
stank too much today
the usual wet dog reek rising
from piles of old damp clothes.

Somebody absolutely steamboats he says on
sweet warm wine
swigged plaincover from a paper bag
squats in a puddle with nothing to sell
but three bent forks   a torn
calendar (last year's)
and a broken plastic sandal.
So we hadn't the stomach for it today.
Oh you could say
we don't deserve a bargain then!
No connoisseur can afford to be too scrupulous
about keeping his hands clean.
There was no doubt   the rare   the beautiful
and the bugle-beaded   the real antique   dirt cheap
among the rags and drunks
you could easily take to the cleaners.

At the Barrows everything has its price
no haggling   believe me
this boy knows his radios.
Pure Utility
and what that's worth these days.
Suddenly the fifties are fashionable
and anything within a decade of art deco
a rarity you'll pay through the nose for.
The man with the patter and all these curtain lengths
in fibreglass is flabbergasted at the bargain
and says so in so many words.
Jesus, every other

arcade around here's
a 'Fire Surround Boutique.'—
and we watch the struggling families:
father carrying hearth home
mother wound up with kids.
All the couples we know fall apart
or have kids.
Oh we've never shouldered much.
We'll stick to small ikons for our home—
as long as they're portable—
a dartboard   a peacock feather
a stucco photoframe.

We queue in a blue haze of hot fat
for Danny's Do-Nuts that grit
our teeth with granules of sugar.
I keep
losing you and finding you—
two stalls away you thumb
through a complete set of manuals for
primary teachers in the thirties.
I rub my sleeve
on a dusty Chinese saucer
till the gilt shows through.
Oh come on   we promised
we'd not let our affection for the slightly cracked
trap us into such expenditure again.
Oh even if it is a bargain
we won't buy.
The stallholder says we'll be the death of her
she says   see January
it's been the doldrums the day.

And it's packing up time
with the dark coming early
and as cold as the river.
By the bus-stop I show you
the beady bag and the maybe rosewood box
with the inlaid butterfly and the broken catch.
You've bought
a record by the Shangri-Las
a pinstripe waistcoat that needs a stitch
it just won't get   and a book called 'Enquire
Within—Upon Everything'.

The raw cold gets colder.
There doesn't seem to be a lot to say.
I wish we could either mend things
or learn to throw them away.

HAFIZ ON DANFORTH AVENUE*

There are no nightingales in this lunchroom, but
I have all these presents wrapped in that cheap
Christmas paper printed with those cardinals
you said sang out too loud.
Waiting for the
last of the breakfast specials I fish out
from the bottom of my handbag your father's
copy of Hafiz you lent me. Old ink
on the flyleaf, the name
that is also your name, the date
and where he bought it.

No place
for a lady here at eleven a.m.
in bitter mid December on the Danforth—all these
Greek men at the counter
on their rooted stools, sallow
under astrakhan, brindled moustaches,
the clack of worrybeads, I catch
a flash of amber and tassels.
A toothpick, a gold filling—
'Tonight I gonna finish one gallon of wine.
Tony makes it great. Forget
the mortgages, the pressure, tonight
if my wife she drives me I can get loaded.'

'A laughing winecup, a tangle
of knotted hair' I tingle
remembering us side by side—I am reading
your old Hafiz, you the New Divan† I
brought with me, somehow linking
Glasgow to Toronto to Teheran.

Later you stretch out,
the book is closed on the carpet
a spiral of tangerine peel on the cover.

In the photograph you showed me Sunday
you are twelve, it is the year
you lived in Baghdad, you
are jug-eared, a proper cropped
North American boy.
There are two Iraqui taxidrivers,
a big Yankee car with
dangling charms of Islam. I can
smell the heat and the petrol.

'The morning breeze is the messenger of Love . . .
The beloved
is sometimes the seller of sweetmeats,
the poet an eloquent sugarloving parrot.'
And today's snowflakes
muffle the mounds of Best Canadian
pumpkins and hubbardsquash outside
next door's greengrocery.
Here, through chromium and steam
the sugar dredger, a plate of lemons,
jellies, sherbert-coloured wedges
of chiffon pie.

The beautiful black waitress
wears a white beanie.

They've written Merry Christmas with glitterdust
on the mirror here in Motorama
beside the poster which says
Cold, Beautiful

Milk.
The young lovers
holding hands under the next table
play on the jukebox
'You don't bring me flowers.'

And to tell you this is easy,
scribbling this was as simple
as the shopping-list it jostles
on the next page of my notebook.
Love, as well as bread and coffee
it says eggplants, olive oil
don't forget
the nutmeg and cinnamon.

*Hafiz: a Persian poet of the fourteenth century, renowned for his
sequence of love lyrics, *The Divan*.
†Edwin Morgan's collection of poems, *The New Divan*.

Today saw the last of my Spanish shampoo.
Lasted an age now that sharing with you,
such a thing of the past is.
Giant Size. The brand
was always a compromise.
My new one's tailored exactly to my needs.
Nonspill. Protein-rich.
Feeds Body, promises to solve my problem hair.
Sweetheart, these days it's hard to care,
But oh oh insomniac moonlight
how unhoneyed is my middle of the night.
I could see you
far enough. Beyond me
how we'll get back together.
Campsites in Spain, moonlight,
heavy weather.
Today saw the end of my Spanish shampoo,
the end of my third month without you.

FOURTH OF JULY FIREWORKS

The guests are gathered.
Boston-Irish Nancy, half in huff
says, 'Better help yourselves,
you all know Mister's timing well enough.'
Aside at me she mutters.
'Millionaires can afford to let things wait.
Honest-to-God Mister would be late
for his own funeral.' Cigarstore Indian,
I hide behind my apron, wait and drink in all I can.

(We don't exist. They pick our trays,
Tom Collinses, Martinis and canapés.)

Oh horror, new England night,
when I fetched the ice down and that snake
looped my feet in the kitchen garden! I still shake.
'Harmless,' says Nancy.
I hear her hiss, 'Some host!
That beggar'll only get here when he's sure he's last.'

Fourth of July. Cape Cod. Dead on cue,
last-man Mister comes running to his barbecue.
Arms flailing like a cricketer's across the lawn
from his 'so English' house with a flame red shirt on.

It's the cocktail hour. The air is still.
Mister gets busy on the charcoal grill.
Social-kissing women, backslapping men
has failed to break the ice. But then
Missiz appears like magic from the dusk.
Cool, ten years his junior, she smells of musk

and 'Madame Rochas'. Two small spots of anger
high on her cheekbones linger.

When Mister says it's done enough
the guests spread ketchup on the fatted calf.
The night hots up. Liquor flows. Listless
couples come alive. A bit apart, restless,
Missiz sways gently on her own
to Glen Miller on the gramophone.
All eyes are on the soignee cling
of this year's leisure favourite, velvety stretch towelling
for patio-party wear. Those purples and electric pinks
'Just far too hectic altogether,' Nancy thinks.

(Ten years with Missiz, Nancy's face
is quite professional, impervious.)

Ice melts in the Martini tray. Midges
drown. The whole night edges
to a thunderstorm. Maybugs big as golfballs thud
as screendoors bounce them. But, after our blood,
divebombing mosquitoes dodge the mesh and slide
in down their own thin whine.
They bite despite insecticide.

All at sea,
white and dayglo orange fins spinnaker the bay.
Music blares
from the jazzed-up clubhouse round the Cape, Cotuit way.
The whole damn town is two thirds empty after Labour Day.
These summer people
migrate to Florida, lock, stock and barrel.
Tonight their parked cars sprawl the drive and trail

behind those his-and-hers coupled custom Cadillacs
like a comet tail.

(Oh I can see it all quite clearly, feeling small
and stone-cold sober. But I do not count at all.)

Out on the lawn the sprinklers, oddly luminous,
sputter like Roman Candles, ominous
as the sudden snap of queer clear light
from one weird streak unzips the dark.
The German Shepherd guard dogs bark.
A wind gets up. These beach-house boards
are flimsier than playing cards.

(Over the bay, like flares
odd rockets go up with a shock of stars.)

Mister drags off his box of fireworks to the shore.
Missiz drains her drink and hits the floor
with someone half her age. His snake-arms slur
around her waist. Eyes glaze. Sentence endings blur.
Missiz ('mutton dressed as lamb')
comes in slowly as the false-calm
lead-slow sea that slicks the beach. Sinatra sings.
The tide ravels up slowly, shelving things.

Raindrops big as bullets dent the roof we all stand under,
watching Canute's fireworks out-rage the storm,
try to steal its thunder.

And for special things
(weddings, school-
concerts) the grown up girls next door
would do my hair.

Luxembourg announced Amami night.
I sat at peace passing bobbipins
from a marshmallow pink cosmetic purse
embossed with jazzmen,
girls with pony tails and a November
topaz lucky birthstone.
They doused my cow's-lick, rollered
and skewered tightly.
I expected that to be lovely
would be worth the hurt.

They read my Stars,
tied chiffon scarves to doorhandles, tried
to teach me tight dancesteps
you'd no guarantee
any partner you might find would ever be able to
keep up with as far as I could see.

There were always things to burn
before the men came in.

For each disaster
you were meant to know the handy hint.
Soap at a pinch
but better nailvarnish (clear) for ladders.
For kisscurls, spit.

Those days womanhood was quite a sticky thing
and that was what these grim sisters came to mean.

'You'll know all about it soon enough.'
But when the clock struck they
stood still, stopped dead.
And they were left there
out in the cold with the wrong skirtlength
and bouffant hair,
dressed to kill,

who'd been
all the rage in fifty eight,
a swish of Persianelle
a slosh of perfume.
In those big black mantrap handbags
they snapped shut at any hint of *that*
were hedgehog hairbrushes
cottonwool mice and barbed combs to tease.
Their heels spiked bubblegum, dead leaves.

Wasp waist and cone breast, I see them yet.
I hope, I hope
there's been a change of more than silhouette.

MIDSUMMER NIGHT

Was that a donkey braying in my dream?
Couldn't make head or tail of it but
it hawhawed itself blue in the face
whatever it was. Still, Confusion's clearly
what's called for in any comedy worth worrying about.
That and Chance
which certainly seems to be
playing its part all right.
So we're laughing?
Get us, half enchanted and undecided
whether or not to give in to it,
wandering the wide woods on such a night like
the wrong pair of ill-met demi-
lovers we most likely are
in far too high a pollen count for
anybody's comfort. This is the
silly season though—you said so yourself—
surely a solstice is a time for going to extremes.
Have a heart though, I've always been
the equinox sort—white nights
and talking till birdsong
are as new a taste to me as the
piney retsina we sat late in the restaurant with,
till one. And still no real dark yet
to go home in.

Earlier, between
the World Cup and Wimbledon the blue
T.V. lights flickered from every douce house
in the solid suburbs we drove through to come
to such a shifting place.

Remember the horses
how silently they moved
from dark woods.
'Would you call this a green glade?' you
asking gravely with a glint,
the lilac haze and three rooks on the long meadow,
that russet shape that changed
we could swear it, and stretched
and lengthened to a fox and back to prick-eared
hare again. Nothing tonight could decide
what form to take.

We are good and strange to one another and no mistake.

STOOGE SONG

How did I get here?
Out of my
streetclothes & into
these sad spangles
having the silken flags of many countries
dragged from between my ears,
the perfect egg
coaxed from my cleavage,
it's undignified.
How did I get here?
The children chorus YOU VOLUNTEERED

& oh yes I
do
seem to remember myself
long ago
safe in the dark on the other side of the orchestra pit
laughing & munching
on those sweets I'd caught, that Buttons threw . . .
then I sort of recall
something about him leaning over the footlights
& me telegraphing furiously
CHOOSE ME CHOOSE ME

& it isn't as if I ever
liked him did I? Surely
I can't have been taken in
by his blackpatent hair & his permanent grin?

Shall I let you into a little secret?
Let me tell you what's what.
Can you keep it under your hat?

There is No Easter Bunny.
There.
Pure illusion & so are
(big gimmick)
those hawks he teases out of handkerchieves
instead of doves.
It wasn't Real Claws
that made such short work
of my
long
kid gloves.

Right on cue he
takes my hand &
I stammer out
that bit about
I HAVE NEVER SEEN YOU BEFORE IN MY LIFE
but I must have my lines all wrong again,
all the people laugh.
& NOW, THE GRAND FINALE
THE LITTLE LADY WILL BE SAWN IN HALF

& oh (here we go again) truly
I have
never had my head so
effectively
separated from my body.
Look I can wriggle my toes, can
wave tinkly fingers from
the four corners of the stage.
I volunteered. It was
all my own idea to come up here.
I smile & smile & smile to show my rage.

THE OTHER WOMAN

The other woman
lies
between us like a bolster.
When I hit out wild she's
insubstantial a
flurry of feathers a mere
sneezing irritant.
When my shaped and hardened words turn
machine-gun
against you she's rock solid
the sandbag you hide behind.

The other woman
lies
when she says she does not want
your guts for her garterbelt.
I send out spies, they say relax
she's a hag she's just a kid
she's not a patch she's nothing to she's
no oil painting.
I'd know her anywhere.
I look for her in department stores, I scan
every cinema-queue.
Sometimes suddenly in some downtown restaurant
I catch her eye
casting crazily around for me.

The other woman
lies
the other side of my very own mirror.
Sweet, when I smile
straight out for you, she
puts a little twist on it, my
right hand never knows what her left is doing.
She's sinister.
She does not mean you well.

From *True Confessions*

VERENA: SECURITY
(Monologue)

See since Derek went up to work there on the Rigs things have been Different. I can't honestly say I really miss . . . Well, basically to tell you the truth it's been . . . better in a way. Definitely. Financially anyway.

I mean we'd never have been able to afford all this. See before with Derek's Other Job, before, on-shore, honest-to-god the Mortgage was a Millstone. Telling you, I thought we'd of been clomping around on the bare floor-boards and sitting on orange-boxes watching a wee black-and-white portable for ever.

But see since he went Up There—well, it's Security, isn't it. Not only did we double-glaze and fitted-Tintawn the whole place from top to bottom but I got my Dream Kitchen! The Exact Units I wanted, eye level grill, Tricity Rotisserie, fully stocked freezer, oh Derek insisted on it.

Money no object.

Not that I bother much with the cooking while he's away. You don't, for yourself, do you? And I'm out a lot, I tend to just slurp down a cup of Slimma-soup, stick a wee dollop of quiche in the microwave or something while I'm waiting for my Carmens to heat up.

Och, just round to my Mother's, basically, just to get out of the house—I've never been one just to sit in listening to the Central Heating switching itself off and on. But see Derek he's that jealous! Honestly, always was, ver-near Divorce Proceedings every time I went out with emdy for a Campari after the Country Dancing . . .

But basically my mother and I have always been very close.

Although I think it's just with us having the None Of A Family ourselves that I've adjusted so well. Derek was telling us only the last time he was home all about his Mate up there on the Rigs. Diver or something, honest-to-god I don't have a *clue* what they actually *do* up there, don't ask me—anyway, seems This Chap had Two Boys, one teenage, the other growing out of anoraks faster than look-at-you so She put pressure on him. How if the boys were to stay-on and get their Highers they needed the Security etc. So he took the job. Seems the Separation put a Strain on the Fragile Fabric of their Marriage and they started to Not Get On. Sexually etc.

Not that I can say either Derek or I have ever had any problems in the Bedroom Compartment. Touch wood. Excuse my French . . . No I can honestly say that Two Weeks On, Two Weeks Off suits me fine just as long as he minds to cut his toenails . . . I mean you've got to keep the Home Fires Burning. Grin and Bear it, make him Feel Welcome—although see when he's up at midnight frying eggs and he spatters grease all over my good ceramic hob I could brain him so I could—but I just tell myself he's Not Home Forever and I bite my tongue.

Anyway, this mate of his and his wife—things went from bad to worse, seems he met this woman from Dundee who travelled down regular on the same train and one day he just Got Off with her and the upshot of the whole thing was a Dear-Jeanette-Letter from Sullom Voe.

Course, as Derek says, his mate is basically a very decent bloke. Good family man. He'll make sure neither the wife nor the two boys ever want for anything.

MIRROR'S SONG
for Sally Potter

Smash me looking-glass glass
coffin, the one
that keeps your best black self on ice.
Smash me, she'll smash back—
without you she can't lift a finger.
Smash me she'll whirl out like Kali,
trashing the alligator mantrap handbags
with her righteous karate.
The ashcan for the stubbed lipsticks
and the lipsticked butts,
the wet lettuce of fivers.
She'll spill the Kleenex blossoms,
the tissues of lies, the matted
nests of hair from the brushes'
hedgehog spikes, she'll junk
the dead mice and the tampons
the twinking single eyes
of winkled out diamante, the hatpins
the whalebone and lycra,
the appleblossom and the underwires,
the chafing iron that kept them maiden,
the Valium and initialled hankies,
the lovepulps and the Librium,
the permanents and panstick and
Coty and Tangee Indelible,
Thalidomide and junk jewellery.

Smash me for your daughters and dead
mothers, for the widowed
spinsters of the first and every war

let her
rip up the appointment cards for the
terrible clinics,
the Greenham summonses, that date
they've handed us. Let her rip.
She'll crumple all the
tracts and the adverts, shred
all the wedding dresses, snap
all the spike-heel icicles
in the cave she will claw out of—
a woman giving birth to herself.

SORTING THROUGH

The moment she died, my mother's dancedresses
turned from the colours they really were
to the colours I imagine them to be.
I can feel the weight of bumptoed silver shoes
swinging from their anklestraps as she swaggers
up the path towards her Dad, light-headed
from airman's kisses. Here, at what I'll have to learn
to call *my father's house*, yes every duster prints her
even more vivid than an Ilford snapshot on some seafront
in a white cardigan and that exact frock.
Old lipsticks. Liquid stockings.
Labels like *Harella*, *Gor-ray*, *Berketex*.
And, as I manhandle whole outfits into binbags for Oxfam,
every mote in my eye is a utility mark
and this is useful:
the sadness of dispossessed dresses,
the decency of good coats roundshouldered
in the darkness of wardrobes,
the gravitas of lapels,
the invisible danders of skin fizzing off from them
like all that life that will not neatly end.